Healing America's Communities

Six Steps I Can Take

By JoeAnn Ballard

Real Life
Stories.
PUBLISHING
SERVICES

Real Life Stories, LLC
PO Box 248
Montreat, NC 28757
828-785-2828
www.ReaLifeStories.com

©2015 Real Life Stories, LLC

Healing America's Communities:
Six Steps I Can Take

JoeAnn Ballard, Sheridan Hill

1. Social Change, 2. Social Sciences, 3. Self-Help

ISBN: 978-0-9905087-0-0

Cover and Interior Design: Cape Fear Images, Inc.

Table of Contents

Introduction

Characteristics of Healthy Community 1

Step One

Believe That Your Contribution Matters 9

Step Two

Identify Your Gifts, Talents, and Resources 13

Step Three

Be a Consistent Donor 17

Step Four

Be a Consistent Servant-Leader 19

Step Five

Engage Children Early 23

Step Six

Identify and Support Emerging Young Leaders 29

You Can Do It 35

Introduction

characteristics
of a healthy
community

We are living in a time when we all sense a fracturing around us, a growing feeling of isolation, a rising of primitive emotions including the fight and flight response, and an increasing need to protect our possessions, resources, and loved ones.

This book offers a path of embarkment for every person in America to bring healing and wholeness to our communities while making them safer. These six steps are guaranteed to make a true difference.

First, we must understand the key—and invisible—attributes of a healthy community:

1. *A healthy community is built, and repaired, from the bottom up.*
2. *A healthy community includes guardians who must be recognized.*
3. *A healthy community is rich with servant/leaders across all socio-economic levels.*

True community is formed from the bottom up and is richly infused with the contributions of guardians and servant/leaders. The existence of these leaders ensures that power and resources are constantly circulating among all members of the neighborhood.

Change, including and especially urban renewal,

will never be successful if the invisible leaders of the neighborhoods are not found, recognized, and consulted.

A healthy community includes shepherds and guardians who are knowledgeable about the community they live in; their invisible connectedness to the whole is recognized and their input is consistently solicited whenever change is being planned and executed. Recent decisions at the federal level have taught us, in retrospect, that every decision that affects the community should be discussed within the community before implementation.. When city planners are envisioning the dismantling and rebuilding of a community, those plans must be explained to the guardians of a community so that they can go door to door explaining to the people what is being planned.

* * *

Most adult Americans alive today have witnessed Supreme Court decisions and federal housing programs completely rearranged housing across the country, and not for the better. While shoveling money at our towns and cities to rejuvenate so-called slums, simultaneously the property rights of the underprivileged were ripped away from them under the guise of eliminating blight.

Across the country, as poorer neighborhoods fell into decline, city leaders saw them as toxic: infested with drugs and promiscuous behavior, bitterness and despair. The only decent thing to do, it was decided, was to buy out property owners and bulldoze the block. It was called *urban renewal*, a misnomer that became a national craze.

Communities of old wooden shacks may have looked like disaster zones to city planners, but they were in fact the very heart blood of communities. There, neighbors lived close enough to talk across their back doors, to borrow a cup of sugar, sit together at the kitchen table, share a cup of coffee, and talk about their concerns. They had small open-air front porches where elders rocked and told their stories, where anyone might call out in a gentle manner to a stranger walking by. In fact, with buildings at a size that accommodated human scale, and with all of the people living together at street level, there were no strangers; anyone you saw might be your cousin.

Urban renewal may have been originally intended

as neighborhood improvement but in too many cases it resulted in entire communities being splintered. People were moved here, and then there, with no place they could really call home.

Unfortunately, "community" was mistaken as a matter of constructing apartments and residences close together. As people were extracted from their communities, they were thrown into sudden grief: they felt the loss of their neighbors in the exact same way that a person experiences the death of a loved one.

As one woman said, "Your neighbors are essentially dead to you. You wake up and the person who was your neighbor yesterday has been moved across town. He doesn't have a phone and can't afford transportation. Before, we had community. We were close to our neighbors. If something bad happened, if your child went to jail, you had someone comforting you and saying, 'Okay, when he gets out, here's what we're going to do.' You had people around you who were stabilizers." What had been community became a situation in which people were planted among strangers in a different part of town, which caused many of them to go into seclusion.

* * *

Change is inevitable. But let us come together to discover how change can be introduced in a way that preserves the good qualities of a place and its people. Long before any major changes are made in a community, the guardians need to be at the table.

If they are to thrive, human beings need connection to the ground and to their neighbors, and they need gardens of some kind, as the best architects in the world continue to point out. "A Pattern Language," published by the Center for Environmental Structure, emphasizes other structural needs that invite and nourish community: streets with live greenery; access to water, pools and streams; access to churches and sacred sites; a balance of private and public places.

A healthy society has diverse communities and provides for them. It is the same as in nature, where diversity is the most vital aspect of the key to survival. A community exists for the total society. The act of building community must be intentional in larger communities, and the needs of children and the elderly must be integrated in a holistic manner rather than as a lower priority. Wherever a person goes, he takes a piece of that community with him. We recognize that there are times when a community must be upgraded or even repopulated, but it must be done with the good of all in mind, or else worse problems will ensue.

Vibrancy in our communities is only possible when, across socio-economic levels, its members understand their value both as servants and as leaders: as servant/ leaders. From the man in the ghetto to the man on Wall Street, from the teenager with time on her hands to the busy soccer mom, all must see themselves as having and continually satisfying an ongoing debt to their community. Margaret Mead famously remarked: "Never doubt that a small group of thoughtful, committed citizens can change the world; indeed, it's the only thing that ever has."

But today's problems call for more than a small group. Today's issues require every one of us to believe that our contributions make a difference and to step forward in whatever way we can. Armed with self-empowerment, we have a powerful tool, but one that is useless if we do not have the eyes to see where our efforts can best be aimed to make the most benefit. When we can perceive and attend to the three components of a healthy community, our efforts can be effective and efficient.

Step 1

Believe That Your Contribution Matters

One bright day at the beach, a rogue tide picked up thousands of live starfish and violently threw them ashore. The beachcombers and sunbathers cocked their heads and spoke to each other about it, all agreeing that it was a shame all those starfish had to die.

A small, lone figure began picking up the stunned creatures and putting them gently back into the knee-deep tide. It was a tedious process, and the shoreline was littered with barely-moving sea stars; and yet, the girl kept at her task.

"That's just a waste of time, honey. They're all going to die anyway," a man called out from his orange and teal beach towel on the sand. "All that trouble you're going to, it doesn't matter. It won't make a difference."

Looking momentarily at the starfish in her hand, the girl said, "It matters to this one," and walked into the surf to set it free.

The first step we must all take in order to bring the United States of America to a greatness it has never seen before is a gesture of self-empowerment. We must believe that each step we take in service to our neighbors, our communities, our towns and cities, is an important step, is an effort that matters.

"The work that reconnects," as activist Joanna Macy calls it, is the most patriotic activity Americans can engage in today. If we are to bring our nation to its true greatness again, we must acknowledge types of empowerment that are quietly surfacing around us, in alleyways and doorways, in homes and in hearts, as an antidote to power-over: the solution is power-with.

As JoeAnn Ballard often points out, a vibrant community needs pilots who can turn this boat around. We all know that we have been heading in the wrong direction for two generations while we, as a country, focused on wealth and consumerism. But today, every adult in America must step forward and say, to yourself and to others: What I do does make a difference.

Step 2

Identify Your Gifts

Seventy-two-year-old Beverly Grant has lived in the same block of Brooklyn for four decades. When she first moved in, back in the 1960s, she was inspired to photograph some of her neighbors, and created what turned out to be stunning portraits that are classic examples of time and place.

Now retired from a desk job and a partially retired from her career as a singer-songwriter-activist, Bev recently got the idea to create a Second Street Reunion. She pulled out the old yellowed photographs and began remembering names, writing them down. A few Facebook connections later, a spark was ignited and soon there were four dozen people excited about coming to—and helping with—the Second Street Reunion.

What joy we might bring to others and ourselves if we took time to discover the resources we each have, both inner and outer resources that might be of help to others. Anything we do that makes connection between members of the community, whether it is an annual potluck or sharing flowers from the garden, is a way of creating wholeness. Everything we do for one person in the community is also an act that benefits the community as a whole.

It is something of a phenomenon that when we share, we have more. A sense of abundance flows from the activity of sharing, just as Jesus showed us with the fishes and the loaves. The lesson is one of faith, one of brotherly love: have faith that when you follow an impulse to help another person, your life will be enriched by it in ways you cannot now perceive.

Step 3

Be a Consistent Donor

In creating the Neighborhood Christian Center in Memphis, Tennessee, I have worked with many donors. Over the course of more than three decades, I have learned firsthand the importance of consistency in those who give.

One individual began giving $300 a month to the NCC, and today, 35 years later, he is still giving. His money has helped to stabilize the entire organization because we could count on it. We could always include it in the budget.

With his initial donation of $300, this man planted a seed. With his continued, regular gifts, he ensured that the seed would grow.

Can you afford $15 a month? If so, simply plan to do it for the rest of your life, and rest assured in the knowledge that your faithful donation does matter.

If a person is a donor, he must be a consistent, lifetime donor. With only a few dollars a month, a schoolbook can be bought for a worthy student; a meal plan can be purchased.

Every little bit helps: simply be consistent.

Step 4

Be a Consistent Servant-Leader

As a child, I had an aunt who faithfully made an annual visit from New Orleans to Lucedale, Mississippi to see the family. This one woman, Aunt Sadie, who came each year at the same time, provided a thread of stability in the fabric of my life, and the lives of the other family members she visited. It's easy for us to say, "It's too much trouble for me to keep it up [visiting, travelling, giving]; no one will notice much difference if I stay home this year." We don't realize that one gesture from one person, consistently offered, can make an important difference in the lives of others.

Every year I could count on Aunt Sadie coming to see us in May. I could feel my body, mind and soul beginning to prepare for her visit. I longed for that visit, and so did all the other cousins. She visited us all. We expected her to be there, and she never let us down. She always made that visit to Lucedale, to Mama's house. Mama cooked, we ate together, and us kids sat around and listened while the grown-ups told stories. When Aunt Sadie was leaving, she was always hugging me as we walked down the steps and out the door to her car. We would stand there with our arms around each other and then she'd say: 'See you later.'

Time is one of the most valuable resources each of us have, and although we live in a time when many people feel that they don't have enough time for their own lives, you can make a difference in your community by choosing to consistently give of your time, even if it is one commitment a year. Perhaps you can help clean up a community once a year, restore an area to cleanliness and create beauty.

Let your face be seen in that neighborhood, even if it is once a year, so those children will make you a part of that community. A sense of community isn't created only by the people living in an area; it also includes everyone who participates in the neighborhood, even once a year.

But what about the times when something goes on that you disagree with? The tendency is to want to withdraw; but before you opt for stepping back, think long and hard about what your absence says.

If you pull back from your family, from people you have begun to mentor, from your church or neighborhood because a situation arises that you don't like, you are starving your community. Be consistent, no matter what.

Step 5

Engage Children Early

We work with three simple stages in child enrichment:

1. *Proximity and engagement,*
2. *Inviting a child to participate and apprentice,*
3. *Leaving the child to accomplish the task on her or his own.*

My husband, Monroe, and I mentored and supported 74 children from the time we were married until the time we lost him to cancer. It was natural for us to step forward to help neighborhood children we saw who needed a hand, who needed an encouraging person in their lives.

Monroe's family shopping procedure was the opposite of what we too often see: kids kicking and screaming in the shopping cart, pulling groceries off the shelf, arguing with their parents. Monroe's policy began with encouraging each child to choose one grocery item he wanted, and the plan would be discussed in advance. Once they entered the store, Monroe would take the child straight to the item he wanted and let him take it off the shelf. For the rest of the shopping trip, the child would remain obedient, while holding onto his Cheerios, or his bar of candy.

The child was engrossed in keeping his special food safe until they could check out, and he was thoroughly engaged in the process. At the checkout counter, Monroe would give each child the right amount of cash to pay for his or her item. Not only were they learning how to behave in a grocery store, they were also learning about money. Monroe made sure the special items were packed on top of the grocery bag, and he'd remind them to carry their special food into the house and then come back and help him with the rest of the bags.

As a child aged, he didn't necessarily want to hold on to his favorite item but instead had become more interested in helping with all of the grocery shopping. When they were ready, he told them, "I'm going to walk alongside while you push the cart and get the groceries.

Monroe felt so certain of his procedure that he liked to tell me, "I could do that with ten children and it would work."

* * *

Each of us must step up to the plate for the sake of our young people. It is all too easy for each generation to discount itself. Young adults might say, "I'm finding my own way," or "I am busy with my own children."

Older adults could rule themselves out with the attitude of, "I've done what I could; I'm tired; I just want to take it easy and please myself for once."

Especially sad is the attitude that some, if not many, Baby Boomers have: "It's all a big mess anyway, and I won't be here in fifty years, so why should I invest my time and money in trying to fix anything?"

Other people are able to find a way to take care of themselves and also engage a child, if even only one child, for the betterment of his or her future.

* * *

All of the problems we now face in America, from generational poverty to the high dropout rate and running all the way up the scale to suicide, are connected to the first six years of a child's life. It does not matter if you don't have money for expensive toys, because enrichment begins with engaging a child with everyday things in everyday ways: stacking pots and pans, folding laundry, sitting in a chair watching the cooking.

I have continued my guardianship role with different children, teaching them the life skills they need. Mentoring is fine, but I'm talking about something that goes deeper. It's closer to love, but I'm not saying you have to love the child you work with. It's really a matter of coaching, but coaching a person for his entire life. That is the kind of in-depth process needed to change a generation.

One of the main crises in this country that hardly anyone is talking about is that Americans have stopped caring about other people's kids. In the past, we always cared about other people's kids; now most people are only concerned with their own children. If we could only turn that around, if we could all agree that we have time to help just one child once a month for the rest of his life, we could turn this country around.

The reason we stress early engagement is that trying to salvage a child from all that has already gone wrong is so much harder than supporting a child who hasn't yet had the time nor inclination to go astray. Comparatively, it takes an enormous amount of money, resources, and time to make a lasting change for the better in the life of a child who has already served time in jail for drug dealing or robbery.

In addition to spending time with a young person, we can also use the conveniences of the Internet and social media such as Facebook and Twitter to let kids know we are thinking of them and are proud of them. Take advantage of this wonderful tool so that you can mentor young people and still go on vacation, still do the things you need to do for your own life.

Step 6

Identify and Support Emerging Young Leaders

In "What the Robin Knows," naturalist Jon Young describes his visit with a Bushman from the remote Kalahari Desert. What the Bushman knows about connectedness offers us an example of what we need to do to enliven and enrich our communities.

"If one day I see a small bird and recognize it, a thin thread will form between me and the bird," he said. "If I just see it but don't really recognize it, there's no thin thread. If I go out tomorrow and see and really recognize that same individual small bird again, the thread will thicken and strengthen just a little. Every time I see and recognize that bird, the thread strengthens. Eventually it will grow into a string, then a cord, and finally a rope. This is what it means to be a Bushman. We make ropes with all aspects of creation in this way."

From this, it is easy to extrapolate the difference between being friendly to the checkout cashier or to your neighbor, whom you see nearly every day, and taking the time to learn his or her name…and using it.

Young people need us to truly "see" them, to take the time to learn their names, and to recognize them again and again, strengthening the bond.

More strategically, in addition to recognizing our

neighbors by name, we need to identify emerging young leaders and shepherd them in whatever way we can, walk them past the cracks in the pavement that will be inevitable with change and growing into young adulthood.

At what age should we look for emerging leaders? I say you should get them at ten years old.

Part of the guardian role in any community is to identify and support emerging leaders, and to take their needs into account when neighborhood change is being discussed. Many problems can be avoided by asking, at the planning stages, how will the children be affected if we move the guardians out of the community?

Children are resilient, but children must be given a strong start, a fighting chance. Every child needs parents or substitute parents, a good school, a welcoming community, and at least a familiarity with spiritual worship or church. All of these components are necessary for a child to thrive.

Many of our servant/leaders are invisible heroes. School teachers are a perfect example of servant/leaders: while they are paid, they also give hundreds of volunteer hours faithfully, year after year, to children who pass through their hands.

Giving once a year, or once a month, is needed, and for some people this will be all you can do. But realize that in this kind of situation, your life is completely separate from the person you are helping. I want to suggest a deeper involvement, where you commit so regularly that this child is part of your life. This child's life is interwoven with yours.

In 2015, I am mentoring nearly 30 young people in a variety of ways. In every case, the child and I commit to the yearlong relationship. I may see the child once a week for an entire day or weekly for an hour (for instance, taking a grandmother to one of her grandchildren's soccer games or other extra-curricular events).

I just build it into my schedule. My grandkids will be with me and involved in the total picture. They're not separate from it. If I pick up John, I am also going to spend time with mygrandchild; I have them both with me. If we are riding in the car, they each hear me talking to the other. They are completely interwoven into my day, my evenings and my weekends. They hear all of my stories. Sometimes he tells his mama, 'I need to go over to Mrs. Ballard's house,' and she drops him off at night and we will have dinner, spend the evening together, and in morning I give him breakfast and take him to school.

If I'm cooking on Saturday, he'll be cooking with me, and on Sunday he'll come over and eat what we cooked. My grandchildren also are included, everyone wants to cook and everyone wants to eat. When there was a crisis in his family, I said to his mama: 'Let him spend time with me.' She was a good mama but she needed another person in his life to be sure he was covered on every side. Kids are not bad; they get bad when they don't have support.

You Can Do It

There are few images more pathetic than of an American complaining about the state of things while doing little or nothing to make a difference. Acting as if you have nothing to offer, acting as if nothing you can do will make a difference is the same as kicking your country while it is down. What one of us believes and does, affects life for all of us, and the hard realities of this universal truth become more apparent every day. We are all in this together. If you are able to choose only one of the six steps in this book, choose this one: believe that your contribution, whatever it is, matters.

www.ingramcontent.com/pod-product-compliance
Lightning Source LLC
Chambersburg PA
CBHW060703280326
41933CB00012B/2285